You Hear With Your Ears

Melvin and Gilda Berger

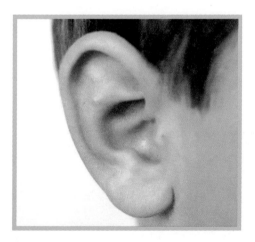

SCHOLASTIC INC.
New York Toronto London Auckland Sydney
Mexico City New Delhi Hong Kong Buenos Aires

Photographs: Cover: David Young-Wolff/PhotoEdit; p. 1: Custom Medical Stock Photo; p. 3: Paul Conklin/PhotoEdit; p. 4: Custom Medical Stock Photo; p. 5: Science Photo Library/Photo Researchers; p. 6: Tom McCarthy/PhotoEdit; p. 7: Mark Richards/PhotoEdit; p. 8: Kathy Sloane/Photo Researchers, Inc.; p. 9: David Sacks/The Image Bank; p. 10: A. Ramey/PhotoEdit; p. 11: Dennis MacDonald/PhotoEdit; p. 12: David Young-Wolff/PhotoEdit; p. 13: Alan Becker/The Image Bank; p. 14: Michael Newman/PhotoEdit; p. 15: Robin Sachs/PhotoEdit; p. 16: A. Ramey/PhotoEdit.

Photo Research: Sarah Longacre

ISBN 0-439-56690-8

12 11 10 9 8 7 6 5 4 3   3 4 5 6 7 8/0
08

Printed in the U.S.A.
First printing, September 2003

You hear with your ears.

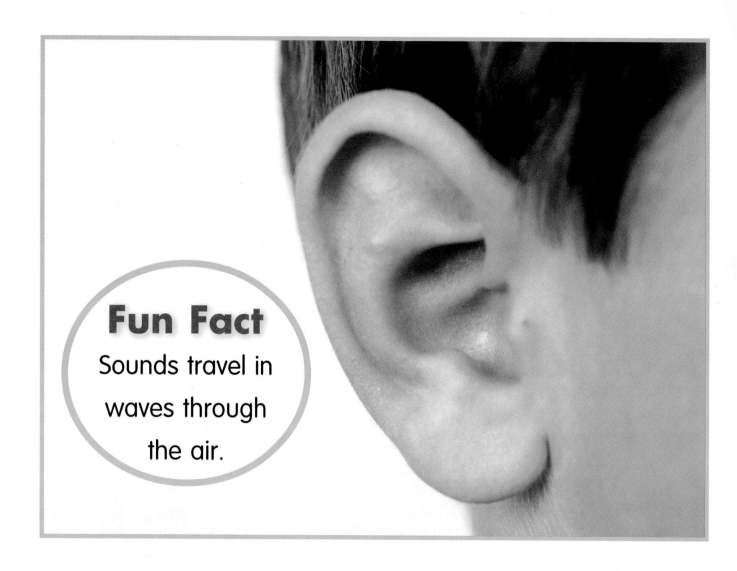

Fun Fact
Sounds travel in waves through the air.

Your ears pick up sounds.

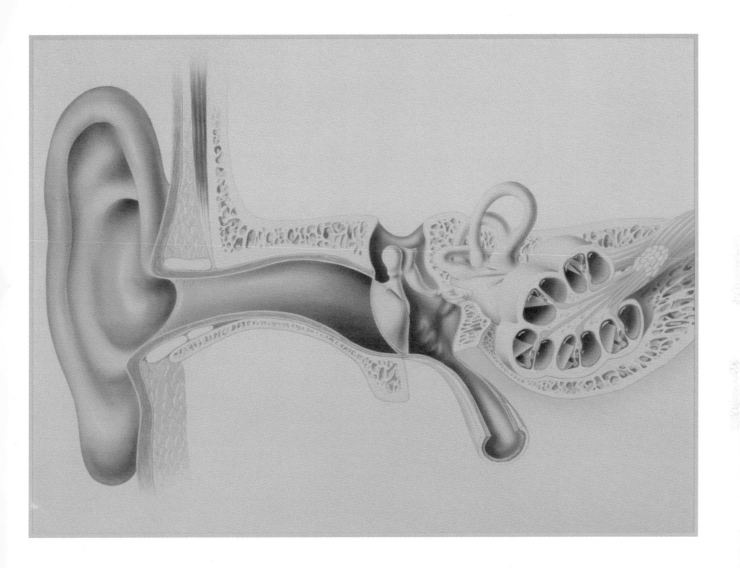

The sounds go inside your ears.

You can hear soft sounds.

Fun Fact

Soft sounds make small waves.

Loud sounds make big waves.

You can hear loud sounds.

You can hear high sounds.

You can hear low sounds.

You can hear sounds
that are near.

Fun Fact

A band near you sounds loud.
A band far away sounds soft.

You can hear sounds
that are far.

Sounds travel through air.

Sounds travel through solids.

Fun Fact
Hearing aids make sounds louder.

Some people need help to hear better.

Other senses can help.

Enjoy what you hear!